Let's Talk About

OVERDOING IT

Let's Talk About
OVERDOING IT

By JOY BERRY

Illustrated by John Costanza
Edited by Orly Kelly
Designed by Jill Losson

GROLIER ENTERPRISES CORP.

Let's talk about OVERDOING IT.

When you *have* too much or *do* too much of one thing, you OVERDO IT.

When you overdo it, you often end up hurting yourself — or other people.

This is because too much of anything can be harmful.

You can overdo it by *eating and drinking too much*. Try not to do this.

Take only a little bit of food at one time.

Eat slowly.

Empty your mouth before you put more food into it.

Do not eat until you are "stuffed."

Do not eat too much of any one thing, especially sweets.

You can overdo it by *staying up too late* and *not getting enough sleep.*

Try not to stay up too late.

With your parents' help, decide when you should go to bed.

One half-hour before bedtime, start getting ready for bed.

Go to bed on time. Don't put it off.

You can overdo it by *being around one person too much.*

Try not to be around any one person too much.

Have several playmates so that you
won't have to play with one person
all of the time.

Learn to play alone so that you
can be by yourself when
you need to be.

You can overdo it by *being in one place too much.*

Try not to be in any one place too long.
If you are getting bored, think about going
someplace else.

- Go into another room if you have been
  in one room too long.
- Go outside if you have been inside
  too long.
- Go to a playground or to a friend's house
  if you have been at home too much.

You can overdo it by *doing one thing too much.* Too much TV is a good example of this.

Try not to watch TV too much.

- Turn the TV set on only when it is
  time for a program that you and
  your parents have decided
  you should watch.
- Turn the TV set off when the program
  is over.
- Try not to watch TV for more than
  one or two hours at a time.

You can overdo it by *being too rough with your toys.*

Try not to be too rough with your toys.

Find out how to use your things properly.

Use your things the way they are supposed to be used so that they will not get broken.

You can overdo it by *playing too roughly with your friends.*

When playing turns into fighting, someone is going to get hurt.

The people, places, and things around you can be wonderful if you use them properly. To use them properly, don't overdo it!